INSTANT GUITAR!
IN FULL COLOR

by Peter Pickow

T0061396

Cover photograph: Randall Wallace

Interior photographs
Page 17: Morena Brengola/allaction.co.uk
Page 5: Andy Cotterill/Camera Press/Retna Ltd, USA
Page 13: John Mather/Retna Ltd/Retna Ltd, USA
Page 51: Mark Shenley/Camera Press/Retna Ltd, USA
Pages 11, 27, 45: J. Scott Wynn/Retna Ltd/Retna Ltd, USA

Interior design and layout: Amy Appleby
Editorial Assistant: Elaine Adam

Order No. AM 975557
US International Standard Book Number: 0.8256.2759.1
UK International Standard Book Number: 0.7119.9679.2

Exclusive Distributors:
Music Sales Corporation
257 Park Avenue South, New York, NY 10010 USA
Music Sales Limited
8/9 Frith Street, London W1D 3JB England
Music Sales Pty. Limited
120 Rothschild Street, Rosebery, Sydney, NSW 2018, Australia

Printed in the United States of America by
Vicks Lithograph and Printing Corporation

Amsco Publications
New York/London/Paris/Sydney/Copenhagen/Madrid

CD Track List

Table of Contents

Getting Started

Welcome to the world's easiest guide to the six-string guitar. This instant guitar course is guaranteed to get you playing right away. Whether you have an acoustic or electric guitar, you'll soon be performing some great songs in different styles.

The color photos and diagrams in your book make it easy to read guitar chords at a glance. These *picture chords* allow you to play songs instantly in a variety of different keys. It's like having a pro show you the exact hand position for each chord before you play it.

Instant Guitar with Picture Chords is fast-moving and fun—and features a great selection of popular songs. Your CD provides a full band arrangement for each song in your book. These backup tracks represent a wide range of styles, including rock, blues, folk, jazz, and Latin music. Your guitar skills will improve rapidly as you practice and play with these professional tracks.

 The numbered CD icons in your book indicate which tracks to play as you progress. Play Track 1 now to hear the introduction.

The picture chords in this book feature the same standard chord diagrams that are found in other songbooks. This means that you will be able to play thousands of new songs on your own after you finish this course. To help you on your way, there's a chord dictionary in the back of this book with basic chords in every key. There's also a list of popular songs for you to explore in future playing sessions.

 Tuning Your Guitar

If your guitar isn't already in tune, take a minute to tune each string with Track 2 of the CD.

○ Pluck the lowest string of your guitar (String 6).

○ Compare this with the E note on the CD.

◉ Adjust the tuning peg until your E note matches this pitch.

Repeat these steps for each of the other strings, from lowest to highest, as you listen to the notes on the tuning track.

STRING	6	5	4	3	2	1
NOTE	E	A	D	G	B	E

Reading Chords

A *chord* is a group of three or more notes that are played together. The pattern of chords in a song is a *chord progression.* Once you know a few chords, you can play hundreds of songs on your own.

Chord Diagrams

A *chord diagram* is like a snapshot of the guitar neck (held vertically). It shows you where to put your left-hand fingers on the strings, and which strings to play.

Take a look at the chord diagram for E7.

- The chord name is shown at the top.
- Numerals mark each finger's position.
- An "o" above a string indicates that you should play that string without fretting, or *open.* (The E7 chord includes all six strings.)

The picture chords in this book are presented horizontally to show the guitar neck in the natural playing position.

Playing with picture chords is easy and fun. It's like having a pro show you how to play.

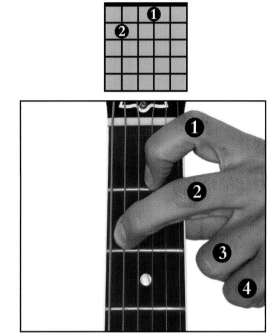

Albert Hammond Jr. of The Strokes

Playing Chords

To play a chord, just fret the strings with your left hand and strum with your right. You can use a pick or strum with the backs of your fingertips. (If you play a left-handed guitar, simply reverse the instructions "left" and "right" throughout this course.)

 **E7 Chord**

Strum the E7 chord now with a downward motion of your right hand across all six strings. Keep your left-hand fingers close to the frets, as shown in the photo.

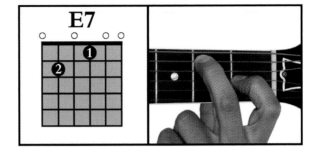

 **A Chord**

Fret Strings 2, 3, and 4 at the second fret. The "x" on String 6 means you should not include it. Strum the top five strings with a downstroke to play the A chord now.

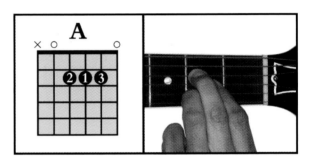

 Strumming

Use a downstroke to play each chord as you change from A to E7, and back again. Count four beats as you play each *whole note*.

- ○ Keep your left thumb behind the neck of the guitar.
- ○ Hold your left wrist low and keep your shoulders relaxed.
- ● Press down with fingertips just behind the fret, not on top of it.
- ○ As you change chords, move your left-hand fingers at the same time and keep them close to the strings.

If you hear buzzing, you're not pressing hard enough with your left-hand fingers—or you're too far away from the fret.

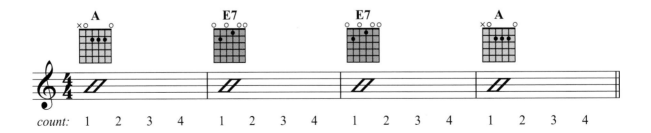

Reading Rhythms

The strum patterns that you play determine the overall rhythm of a song. Each song in this book features one or two distinctive patterns. These strums are made up of notes and rests.

In the last track, you played a series of *whole notes,* which last for four beats each. Take a minute now to learn how some other notes and rests are counted.

Notes and Rests

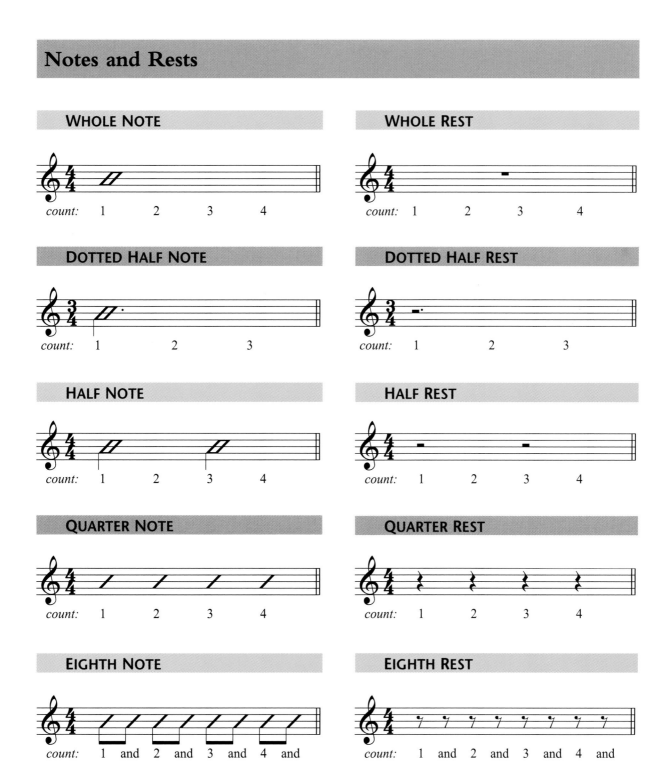

WHOLE NOTE

count: 1   2   3   4

WHOLE REST

count: 1   2   3   4

DOTTED HALF NOTE

count: 1   2   3

DOTTED HALF REST

count: 1   2   3

HALF NOTE

count: 1   2   3   4

HALF REST

count: 1   2   3   4

QUARTER NOTE

count: 1   2   3   4

QUARTER REST

count: 1   2   3   4

EIGHTH NOTE

count: 1 and 2 and 3 and 4 and

EIGHTH REST

count: 1 and 2 and 3 and 4 and

Strum a Waltz

Now that you know two basic chords, you're ready to play a song. "Down in the Valley" has a lilting melody and simple harmony. It is called a *waltz* because it has three beats in every *bar*. To play the guitar part for this song, you will alternate between the A and E7 chords with a simple waltz strum.

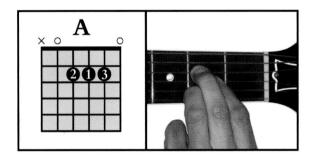

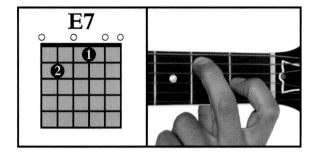

 ## Waltz Strum

Every waltz is counted in three, with three beats in each bar. Listen to Track 6 now to hear "Down in the Valley" with the guitar part shown below.

For this strum, you'll play a chord on the first beat of each bar, and let it ring out for three full beats. Try this now as you play "Down in the Valley" twice through with Track 7.

∏ = downstroke

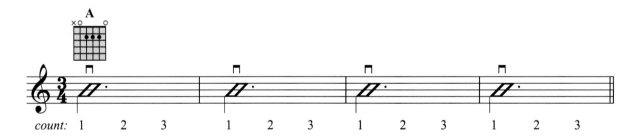

Down in the val - ley,_____ The val - ley so low,_____

Hang your head o - ver,_____ Hear the wind blow._____

Hear the wind blow, dear,_____ Hear the wind blow,_____

Hang your head o - ver,_____ Hear the wind blow._____

2. Roses are red, dear, Violets are blue,
   Angels in heaven Know I love you.
   Know I love you, dear, Know I love you,
   Angels in heaven Know I love you.

Play the Blues

Most blues songs feature three basic chords. Once you learn the D chord, you'll be able to play any traditional blues in the Key of A.

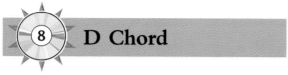

D Chord

Strum the highest four strings to play this chord. Once you can play the D chord, practice changing from D to A to E7 until you can move smoothly between chords.

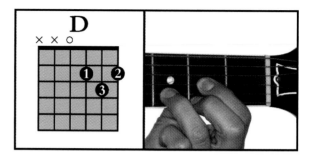

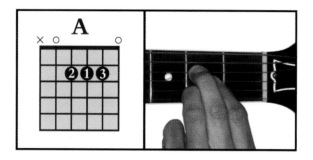

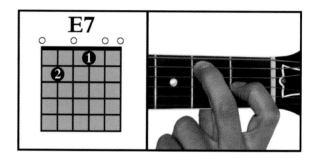

Blues Strum

The blues is often counted in four, with four beats in each bar. Listen to Track 9 now to hear a steady blues strum played throughout "Good Morning Blues."

To play this strum, use a downstroke on every other beat for two bars—then downstroke on every beat for two bars. Repeat this pattern as you play the chords to "Good Morning Blues" with Track 10.

Well, good morn-ing, blues, blues, how do you do? Well, good

morn-ing, blues, blues, how do you do? Well, I'm

←*play first time only*

do-ing all right, say, good morn-ing, how are you?

2. I got up this morning, blues walked 'round my bed,
   I got up this morning, blues walked 'round my bed,
   Went to eat my breakfast, and the blues was in my bread.

Jack White of the White Stripes

Explore Dixieland Jazz

Many early jazz songs also use the three blues chords you have already learned. "When the Saints Go Marching In" is an old favorite in New Orleans which became a big hit for Louis Armstrong. Take a minute to listen to the strum pattern shown below, then play this jazzy spiritual with the CD.

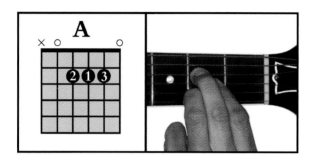

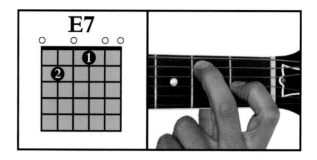

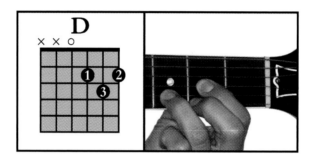

 Dixieland Strum

"When the Saints Go Marching In" is counted in four, with four beats in each bar. Listen to the guitar part in this song on Track 11.

For this strum, don't play on the first beat for two bars, then strum on every beat for the next two bars. Repeat this pattern as you play this great jazz standard twice through with Track 12.

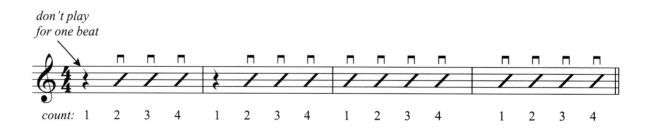

12

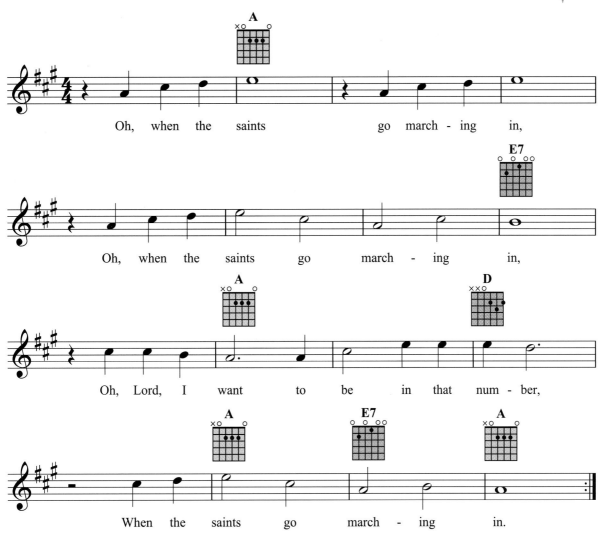

Oh, when the saints go march - ing in,

Oh, when the saints go march - ing in,

Oh, Lord, I want to be in that num - ber,

When the saints go march - ing in.

Nicholaus Arson of The Hives

Play Latin-Rock

"La Bamba" is a hot Latin dance tune that became a big hit for both Ritchie Valens and Los Lobos. You can play this song using just three chords. Many classic rock tunes use this same chord pattern, including "Good Lovin'" and "Twist and Shout."

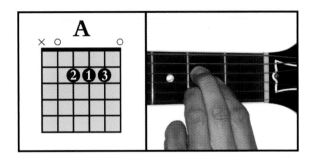

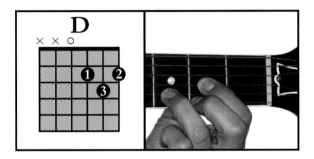

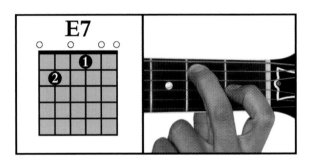

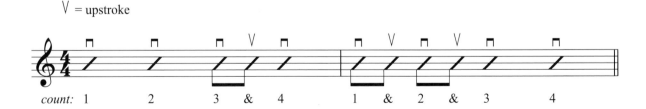

13 Rock Strum

"La Bamba" is counted in four, with four beats in each bar. Play Track 13 to hear the guitar part in this song—and get a feel for the steady, dance rhythm.

When you play this powerful strum with Track 14, use both down-strokes and upstrokes to create a fast rock beat.

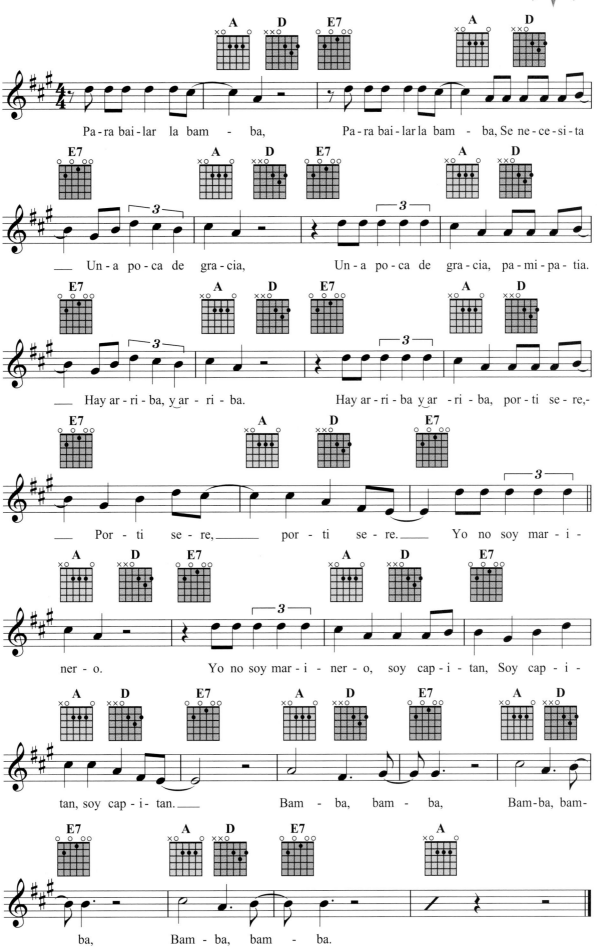

Strum a Country Song

So far, you've played four songs in the Key of A using the A, D, and E7 chords. Get ready now to learn two new chords and a country strum so that you can play "Tom Dooley" in the Key of C.

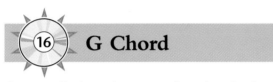

C Chord

Strum the five highest strings when you play the C chord.

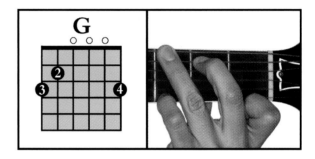

G Chord

Strum all six strings to play the G chord. Once you can play the C and G chords, practice moving smoothly from one chord to the other.

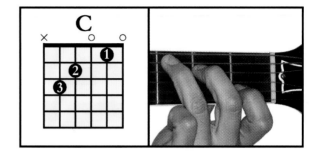

Country Strum

"Tom Dooley" is counted in four, with four beats in each bar. Listen to the guitar play this simple, steady strum in the arrangement on Track 17.

When you play this strum with Track 18, use both downstrokes and upstrokes to create a relaxed country rhythm.

Met her on the moun - tain, Asked her to be my wife.

Met her on the moun - tain, There I took her life.

Chorus

Hang down your head, Tom Dool - ey, Hang down your head and cry.

Hang down your head, Tom Dool - ey, Poor boy, you're bound to die.

Chris Martin of Coldplay

Explore African Rhythms

African music is known for its compelling rhythms and danceability. These qualities are also integral to blues, rock, and jazz. In the South African song "Wimoweh," the melody has a lively, galloping rhythm. Once you've learned the D7 chord and a new strum, you'll be ready to play this great song.

 **D7 Chord**

Like the D chord, the D7 chord is played on the four highest strings. Once you can play D7, practice changing back and forth from this chord to C and G.

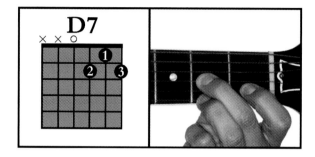

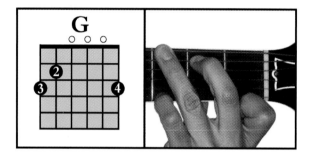

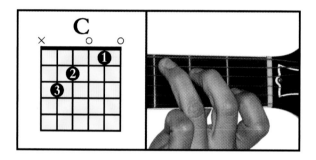

 Galloping Strum

"Wimoweh" has six beats in each measure, and is counted in six. Listen to the guitar part on Track 20 to hear the galloping strum. Notice that its rhythm is the same as the rhythm of the melody.

When you play the guitar part with Track 21, use alternating down-strokes and upstrokes to add some rhythmic swing.

A - wim - o - weh, a - wim - o - weh, a - wim - o - weh, a - wim - o - weh, A -

wim - o - weh, a - wim - o - weh, a - wim - o - weh, a - wim - o - weh, A -

wim - o - weh, a - wim - o - weh, a - wim - o - weh, a - wim - o - weh, A -

wim - o - weh, a - wim - o - weh, a - wim - o - weh, a - wim - o - weh,

Wim - o - weh!

Play Caribbean Style

Reggae and calypso music typically combine simple harmony with lilting rhythms. Many Caribbean songs emphasize the *offbeats* (which fall before and after the primary beats of the bar). Called *syncopation,* this technique is central to other African-influenced music, including blues, jazz, and rock.

 ## A7 Chord

Strum the highest five strings when you play this chord. Practice moving smoothly from D to A7, and back again. Also practice moving from D to G.

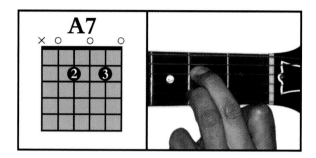

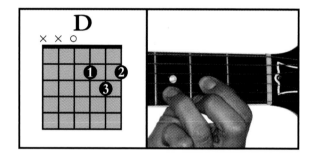

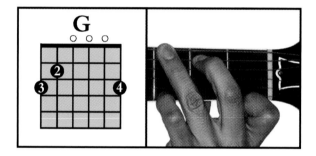

 ## Syncopated Strum

Listen to Track 23 to hear the guitar play this gentle island rhythm in the chorus of "Sloop John B."

When you play the complete song with Track 24, use an upstroke on each of the first two offbeats (which are counted as "and").

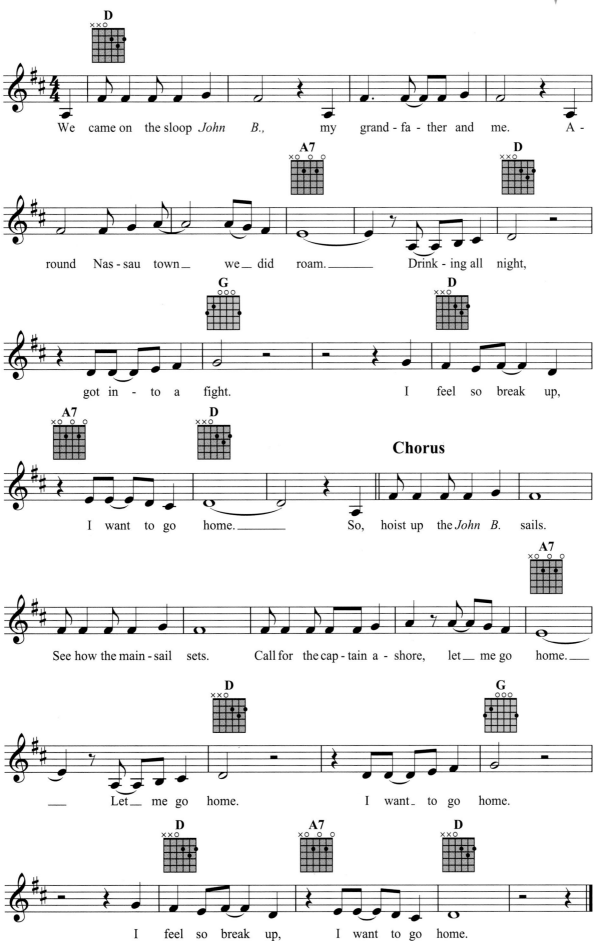

Perform a Blues Ballad

"Frankie and Johnny" is an old-time blues song with a syncopated melody. Because it tells a story, this ballad has quite a few verses. The CD accompaniment plays seven times so you can perform them all.

 G7 Chord

Like the G chord, G7 is played using all six strings. Once you've learned G7, practice changing back and forth from this chord to each of the chords below.

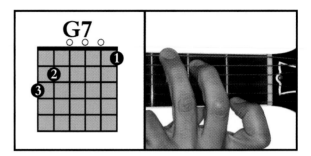

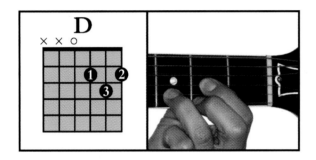

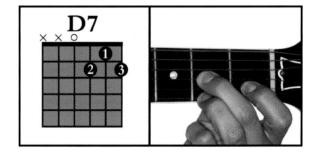

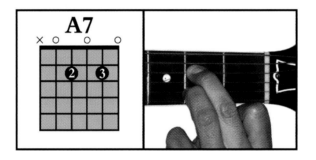

 Syncopated Blues Strum

The curved line in this strum is called a *tie.* This means you should play the two linked notes as one note, with a single strum. Listen to the first verse of "Frankie and Johnny" on Track 26 to hear this syncopated guitar part.

Once you can play this strum smoothly with Track 27, try creating your own variations on additional verses of "Frankie and Johnny."

Frank - ie and John - ny were lov - ers. Oh, Lord - y how they could love.

Swore to be true_ to each oth - er. True as the stars a - bove. He was her man,

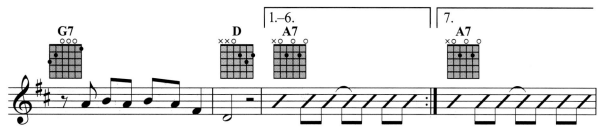

But he was do - ing her wrong.

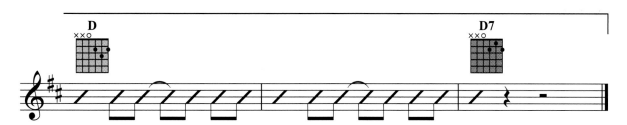

2. Frankie went down to the corner,
Stopped in to buy her some beer.
Says to the big bartender,
"Has my Johnny man been here?"
He was her man,
But he was doing her wrong.

3. "Well, I ain't going to tell you no story,
Ain't going to tell you no lie:
Johnny went by 'bout an hour ago
With a girl named Nellie Bligh,
He was your man,
But he's doing you wrong."

4. Frankie looked over the transom
To see what she could spy.
There sat Johnny on the sofa
Just loving up Nellie Bligh.
He was her man,
But he was doing her wrong.

5. Frankie got down from the high stool,
She didn't want to see no more.
Rooty-toot-toot, three times she shot
Right through that hardwood door.
He was her man,
But he done her wrong.

6. "Oh, roll me over so easy,
Roll me over so slow,
Roll me over easy, boys,
Why did she shoot so low?
I was her man,
But I done her wrong."

7. The sheriff arrested poor Frankie,
Took her to jail that same day.
He locked her up in a dungeon cell
And threw the key away.
She shot her man,
'Cause he was doing her wrong.

Strum a Folk Hymn

"Amazing Grace" is a beautiful folk hymn that is more popular today than ever. Many artists have recorded this song in a wide range of musical styles. You'll find it easy to play this one right away, as you already know all the chords. Notice that when you change from G to G7, you don't need to move your second and third fingers.

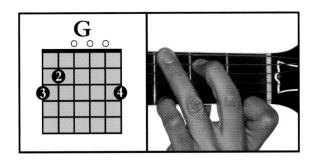

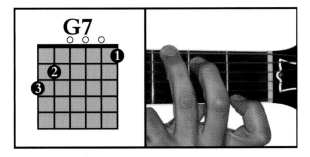

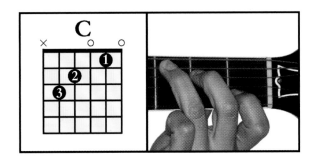

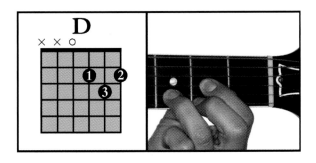

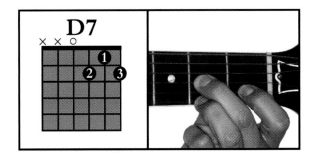

 Waltz Strum

Listen to the first verse of "Amazing Grace" on Track 28. The steady waltz strum provides a gentle setting for this song.

Once you can play the strum smoothly, try creating your own variations for additional verses as you play along with Track 29.

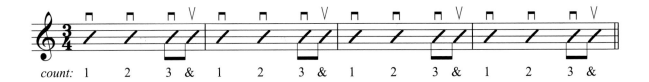

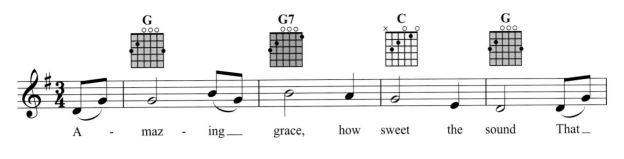

A - maz - ing___ grace, how sweet the sound That___

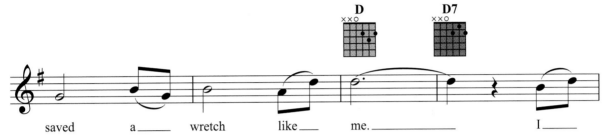

saved a___ wretch like___ me._____ I___

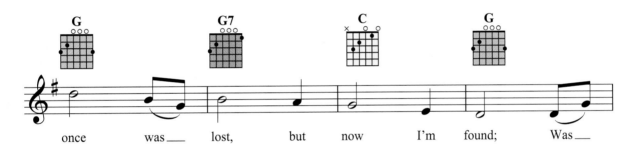

once was___ lost, but now I'm found; Was___

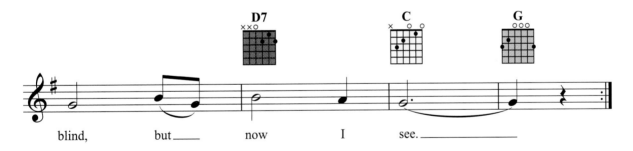

blind, but___ now I see._____

2. 'Twas grace that taught my heart to fear,
   And grace that fear relieved.
   How precious did that grace appear
   The hour I first believed.

3. Through many dangers, toils, and snares
   I have already come.
   'Tis grace that brought me safe thus far,
   And grace will lead me home.

4. When we've been there ten thousand years,
   Bright shining as the sun,
   We've no less days to sing God's praise
   Then when we first begun.

Discover Blues-Rock

"C.C. Rider" is a traditional blues which became a hit for several rock artists. While the song features a basic blues melody and harmony, the strong and steady strum in the guitar part is pure rock and roll.

 **B7 Chord**

Strum the top five strings to play this chord. Practice moving back and forth from B7 to E7 and A7. You don't need to move your second finger to change from B7 to E7.

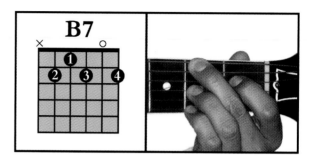

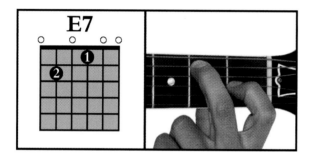

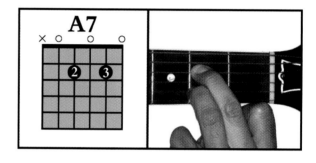

 Blues-Rock Strum

Listen to the guitar part play one verse of "C.C. Rider" on Track 31. This strum uses *sixteenth notes* to create a driving rock beat. Sixteenth notes are easy to count because they are twice as fast as eighth notes.

When you play this strum with Track 32, use repeated downstrokes to create a powerful rock setting for "C.C. Rider." To produce an authentic blues-rock sound, try playing just the lowest three or four strings on each chord.

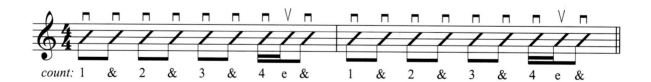

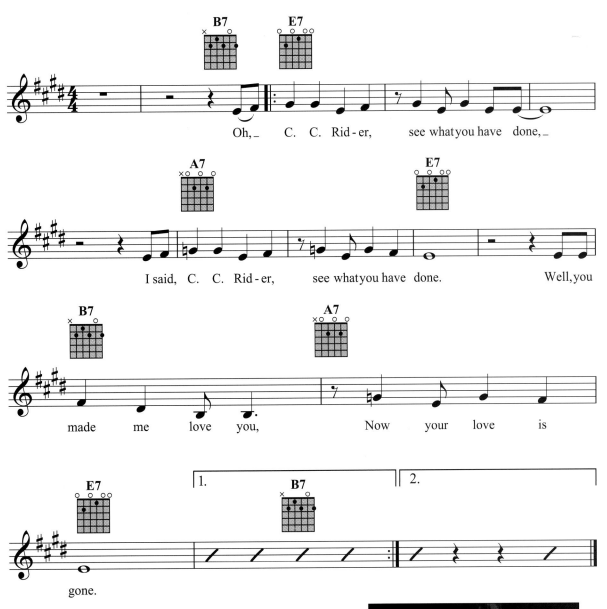

Oh,_ C. C. Rid-er, see what you have done,_

I said, C. C. Rid-er, see what you have done. Well, you

made me love you, Now your love is

gone.

2. Oh, C. C. Rider, I need you by my side,
   I said, C. C. Rider, I need you by my side,
   You're the only one who keeps me satisfied.

Charlotte Hatherley of Ash

Strum an Irish Ballad

"Danny Boy" has a lilting melody and a beautiful, rich harmony. Once you've learned the E chord, take some time to practice the strum for this great Irish song.

 33 **E Chord**

Strum all six strings to play the E chord. Practice moving back and forth from E to each of the chords below. You can move from E to E7 by just lifting your third finger.

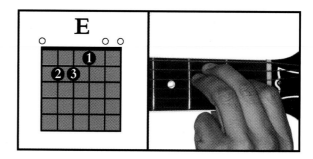

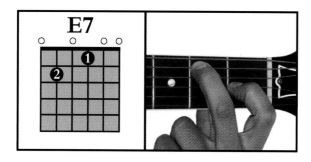

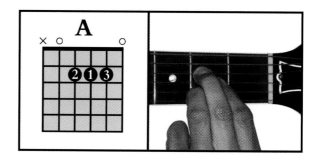

 34 **Bass-Chord Strum**

The guitar part for "Danny Boy" features a new accompaniment style. Listen to this bass-chord strum in the arrangement on Track 34.

When you play the song with Track 35, you'll pluck single bass notes on String 6 (before the E and E7 chords) and String 5 (before the A and B7 chords). If you are not using a pick, pluck single notes with your thumb and strum the chords with your other fingers.

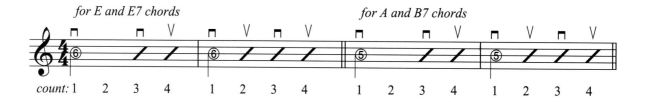

"Rock Island Line" is an old country blues with a driving melody. First play the C7 chord, then check out the two strums. Using syncopation and damping, you can create a great chugging rhythm for this classic train song.

 ## 36 C7 Chord

Strum the top five strings to play this chord. Then practice changing back and forth from C7 to G7 and D7.

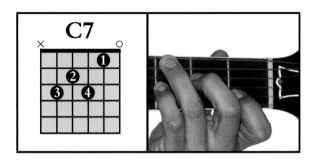

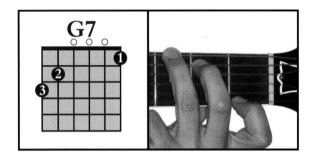

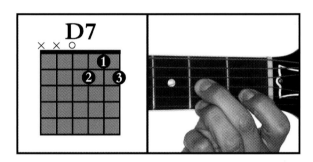

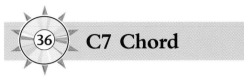 ## 37 Syncopation and Damping

Listen to the guitar part of "Rock Island Line" on Track 37 to hear two different blues strums. You'll play this syncopated strum during Lines 1, 2, and 3 of "Rock Island Line." Remember to play the two tied notes as a single note.

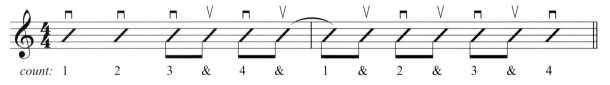

Use this next strum to play Lines 4 and 5 of "Rock Island Line." On Beat 2 of each bar, muffle the strings with your left hand while you strum with your right. Called *damping*, this traditional blues technique produces a rhythmic thud.

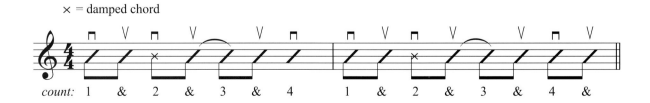

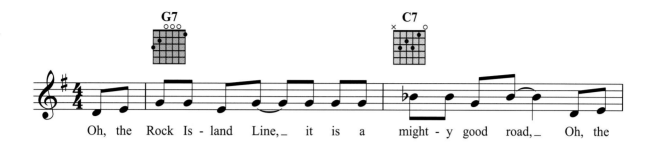

Oh, the Rock Is - land Line, __ it is a might - y good road, __ Oh, the

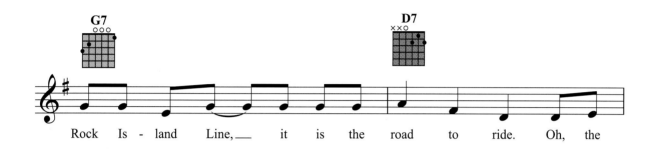

Rock Is - land Line, ___ it is the road to ride. Oh, the

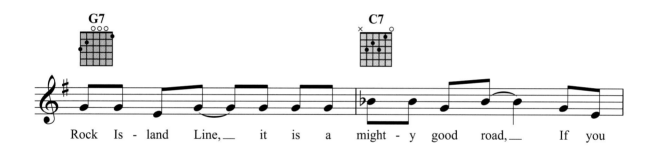

Rock Is - land Line, ___ it is a might - y good road, ___ If you

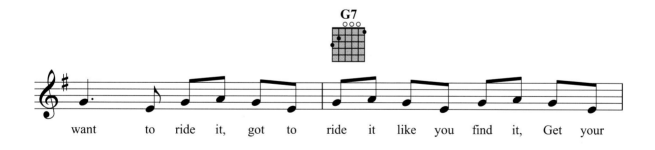

want to ride it, got to ride it like you find it, Get your

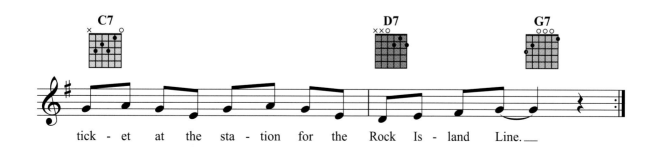

tick - et at the sta - tion for the Rock Is - land Line. __

Explore Folk-Rock

"Kumbaya" is an African-American spiritual that sounds great in a soft rock setting. Once you've mastered the F chord and strums, play this beautiful song with the CD tracks.

 F Chord

Lay your index finger across all strings to *bar* at the first fret. Place your other fingers as shown. Once you can play F clearly, practice moving back and forth to C and G7.

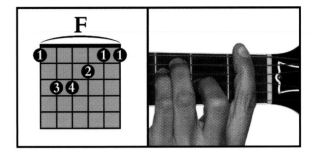

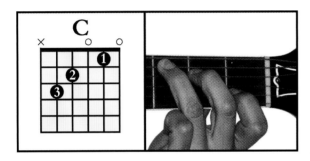

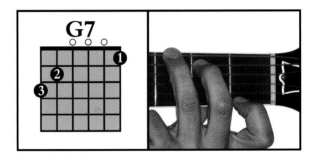

 Rolled Chords

Listen to the guitar part in "Kumbaya" on Track 40 to hear two contrasting strums. The first strum provides a nice introduction—and is also played in the first and second endings (marked *1* and *2*).

A wavy line tells you to play a *rolled chord* in the first beat of each bar. As you strum "Kumbaya" with Track 41, play each rolled chord slowly, so that each note sounds individually. Start each rolled chord just before the beat, so that the chord sounds fully on the first beat.

Play this gentle, syncopated strum during each verse of "Kumbaya."

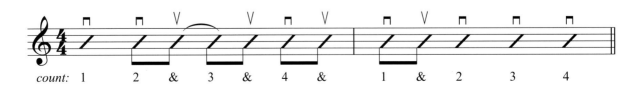

Introduction

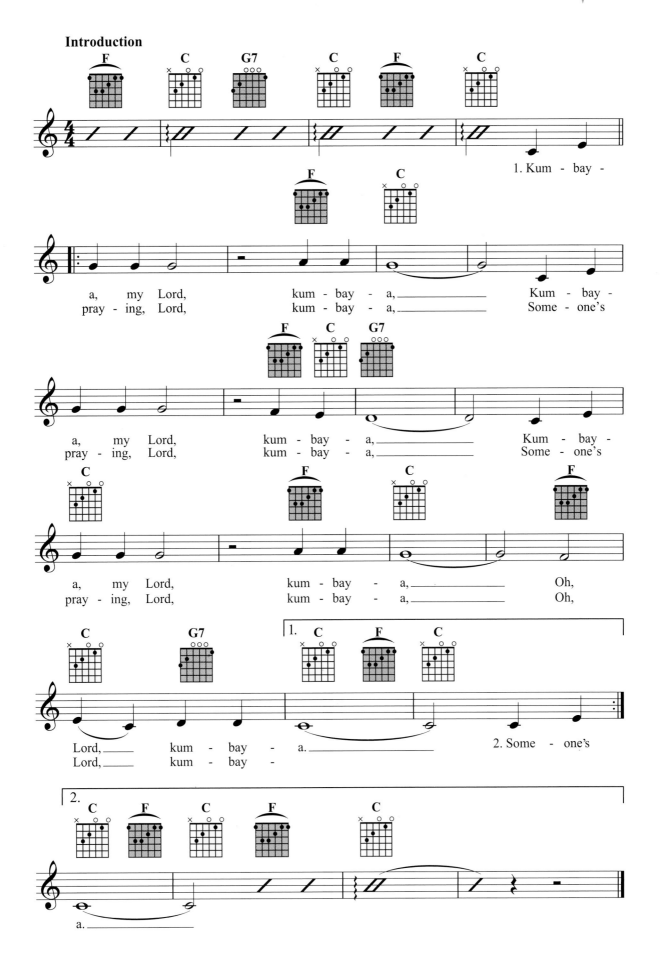

Play a Popular Ballad

You already know all of the chords needed to play "Oh, Susanna."
This great song by Stephen Foster became a hit for James Taylor in
the 1970s. Listen to the syncopated pop strum, then play this ballad
with the CD.

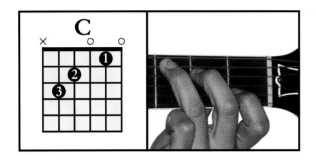

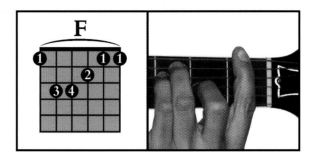

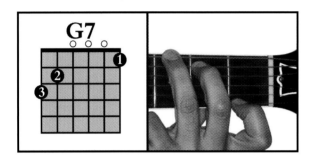

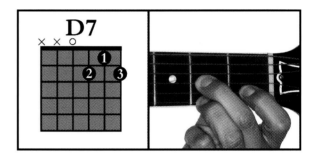

 **Pop Strum**

This strum features a tied note in the second bar. This creates a nice
bit of syncopation in the guitar part for "Oh, Susanna" on Track 42.

Play "Oh, Susanna" twice through with Track 43. Once you can play
this strum smoothly, feel free to explore other strums that comple-
ment the song's easy pop feel.

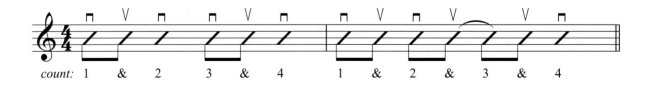

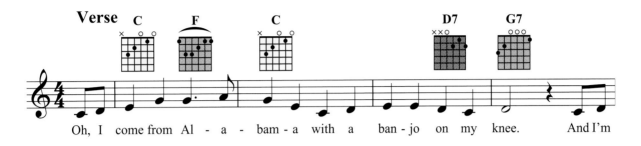

Oh, I come from Al - a - bam - a with a ban - jo on my knee. And I'm

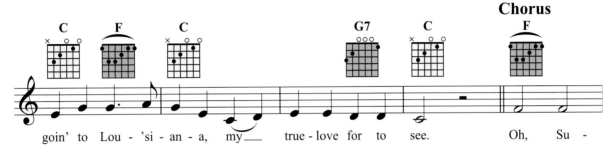

goin' to Lou - 'si - an - a, my___ true - love for to see. Oh, Su -

san - na, oh, don't you cry for me. For I

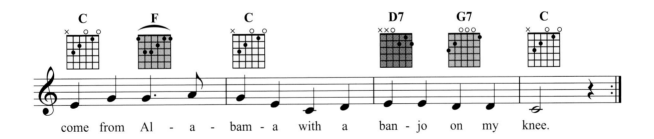

come from Al - a - bam - a with a ban - jo on my knee.

2. Oh, it rained all night the day I left, the weather it was dry,
The sun so hot, I froze to death, Susanna don't you cry.

Chorus

Accompany a Singer

Many guitarists are also singers and use the instrument to accompany themselves. If you haven't been singing along with the CD, take the time now to practice this important skill. Remember, there is a singer inside *everyone,* so really sing out as you strum the guitar accompaniment for "Michael, Row the Boat Ashore" in the Key of C.

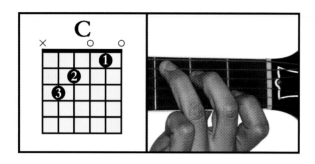

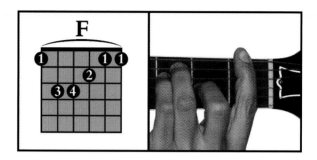

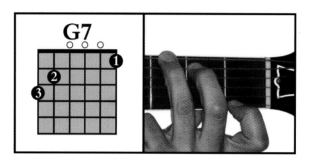

 ## Contrasting Strums

A good accompanist uses different rhythms to keep an arrangement interesting. Listen to the guitar part for "Michael, Row the Boat Ashore" on Track 44 to hear two contrasting strums.

When you play the song with Track 45, use this strum during the first half of each verse.

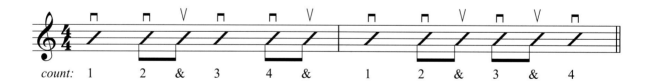

Switch to this syncopated strum for the second half of each verse.

MICHAEL, ROW THE BOAT ASHORE

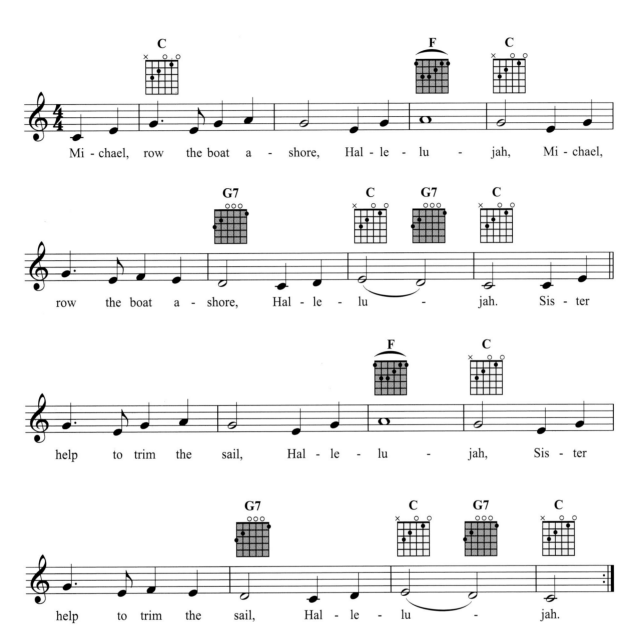

Mi - chael, row the boat a - shore, Hal - le - lu - jah, Mi - chael,

row the boat a - shore, Hal - le - lu - jah. Sis - ter

help to trim the sail, Hal - le - lu - jah, Sis - ter

help to trim the sail, Hal - le - lu - jah.

2. Jordan's river is chilly and cold, Hallelujah,
Chills the body but not the soul, Hallelujah.
Jordan's river is deep and wide, Hallelujah,
Milk and honey on the other side, Hallelujah.

Transpose a Song

It's good to be able to play a song in different keys. You just played "Michael, Row the Boat Ashore" in the Key of C. Get ready now to sing and play this song in the Key of G using the same strums. (You'll know pretty quickly which key works better for your vocal range.)

Read up on the capo to learn how you can easily transpose music to other keys. Then play "Michael, Row the Boat Ashore" again in the Key of G with Track 46.

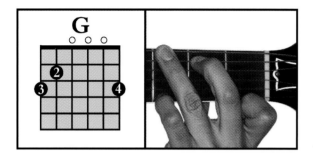

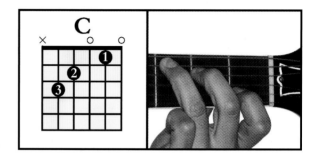

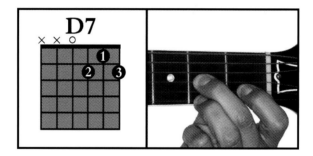

THE CAPO

The *capo* is a bar that you clip onto a fret of the guitar neck. This allows you to quickly transpose a song without changing the chord fingerings. If you don't already own a capo, you should consider buying this handy guitar accessory.

Capos come in a variety of different styles. Although the all-metal capo is stronger, some guitarists feel that this type can scratch the back of the guitar neck. The most commonly used capo is the elastic-band type.

If you have a capo, try transposing "Michael, Row the Boat Ashore" from the Key of G to one of the following new keys.

- Capo Fret 1 to raise the key from G to G♯ (one half step).

- Capo Fret 2 to raise the key from G to A (one whole step).

- Capo Fret 3 to raise the key from G to A♯ (one-and-a-half steps).

- Capo Fret 4 to raise the key from G to B (two whole steps)

2. Jordan's river is chilly and cold, Hallelujah,
   Chills the body but not the soul, Hallelujah.
   Jordan's river is deep and wide, Hallelujah,
   Milk and honey on the other side, Hallelujah.

Strum a Minor Blues

Here's a famous blues from New Orleans that's spent plenty of time on the charts. The repeated chord pattern Am-C-D-F provides a compelling backdrop for this Southern blues in the Key of A Minor. Once you are familiar with the chords and strum, play "House of the Rising Sun" with the CD.

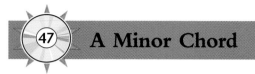

A Minor Chord

Strum the top five strings to play the A minor chord. Practice playing Am-C-D-F a few times, then move from Am to E7, and back again.

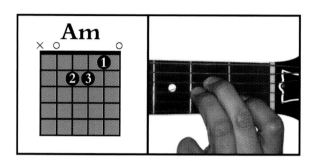

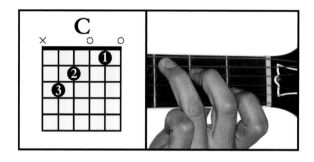

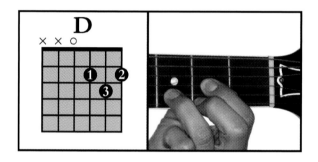

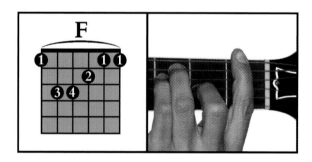

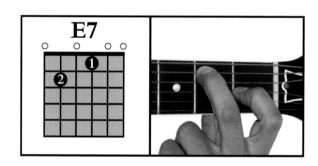

Backbeat Strum

The guitar part on Track 48 features a *backbeat,* which is a heavily accented beat in the middle of the bar.

You will play this backbeat strum throughout "House of the Rising Sun" with Track 49 to create a relentless blues feel.

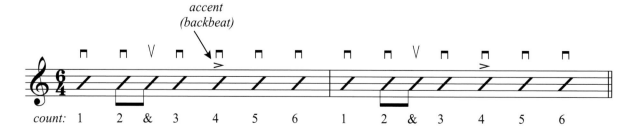

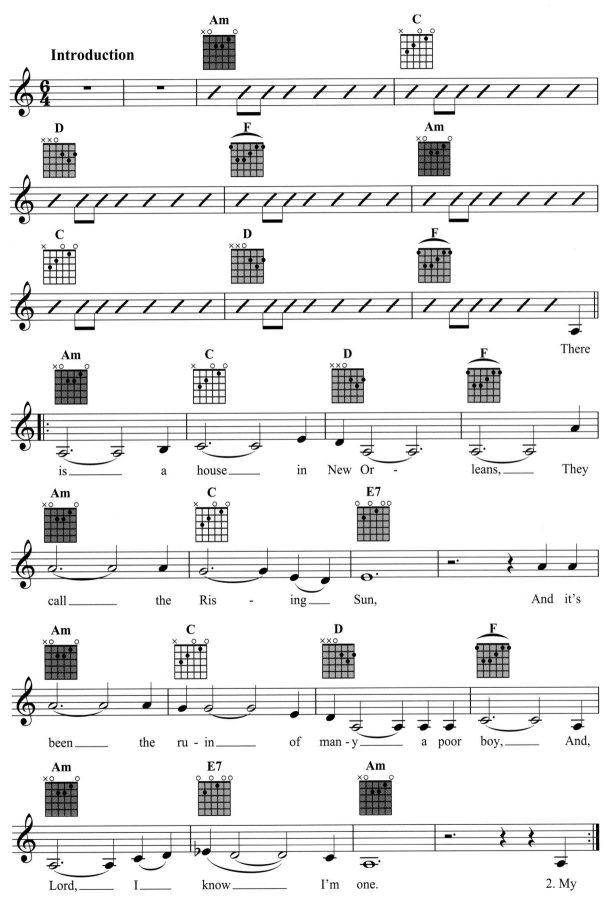

2. My mother was a tailor,
   She sewed my new blue jeans.
   My father was a gambling man
   Way down in New Orleans.

3. Oh, mothers, tell your children
   Not to do what I have done,
   To live in sin and misery
   In the House of the Rising Sun.

4. I'm going back to New Orleans,
   My race is almost run.
   I'm going to spend the rest of my life
   Beneath that Rising Sun.

Play a Minor Ballad

"Scarborough Fair" is a traditional English ballad that Simon and Garfunkel popularized in the 1970s. This haunting melody sounds great in the Key of D Minor with a gentle bass-chord strum.

D Minor Chord

Strum the top four strings when you play this D minor chord. Practice changing back and forth from D minor to each of the chords below.

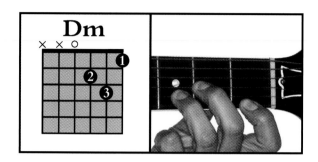

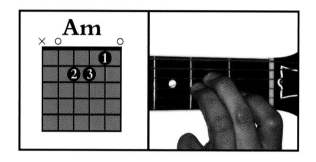

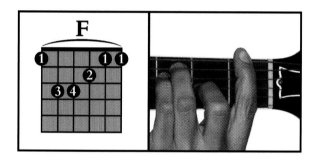

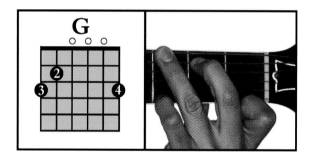

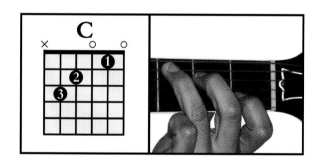

Bass-Chord Strum

The guitar part for "Scarborough Fair" on Track 51 features a bass-chord accompaniment. When you play this strum with Track 52, use single bass notes on String 4 (before the D minor chord), on String 5 (before the A minor and C chords), and on String 6 (before the F and G chords).

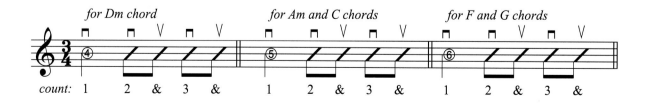

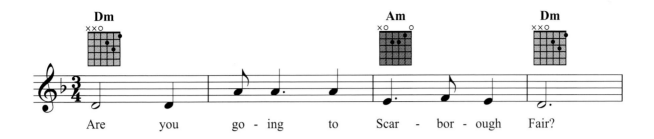

Are you go - ing to Scar - bor - ough Fair?

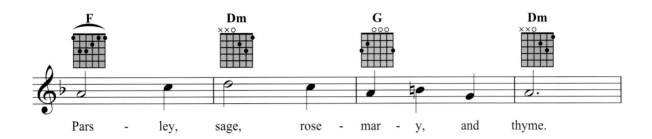

Pars - ley, sage, rose - mar - y, and thyme.

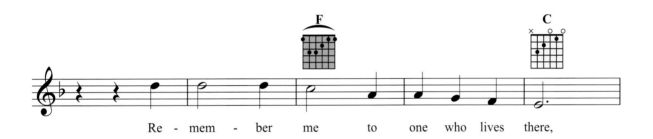

Re - mem - ber me to one who lives there,

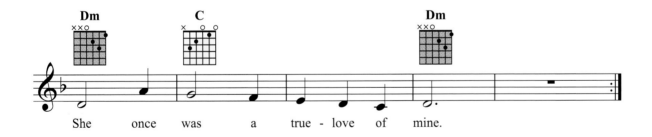

She once was a true - love of mine.

2. Tell her to make me a cambric shirt,
Parsley, sage, rosemary, and thyme,
Without a seam or fine needlework,
Then she'll be a truelove of mine.

3. Oh, will you find me an acre of land,
Parsley, sage, rosemary, and thyme,
Between the sea foam and the sea sand,
Or never be a truelove of mine.

4. And when you've done and finished your work,
Parsley, sage, rosemary, and thyme,
Then come to me for your cambric shirt,
And you shall be a truelove of mine.

5. Are you going to Scarborough Fair?
Parsley, sage, rosemary, and thyme,
Remember me to one who lives there,
She once was a truelove of mine.

Celebrate the Holidays

The holiday season is always a great time for friends to make music together. Here's a wintertime song that everyone loves to sing. Once you know the chords and strum, play "Jingle Bells" with the CD.

 E Minor Chord

Like the E and E7 chords, the E minor chord is played using all six strings. Practice playing G-D-E7-A7-D a few times. Then try this pattern: G-D-Em-A7-D

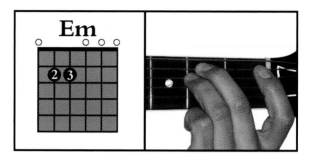

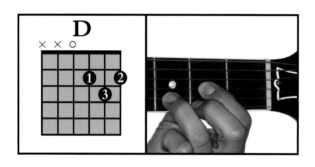

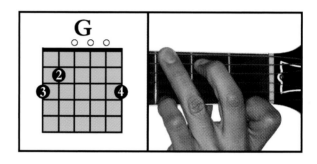

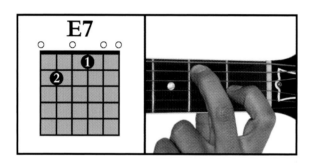

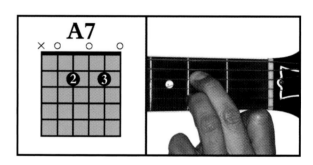

Accented Strum

Listen to the guitar part on Track 54 to hear how this strum provides a festive rhythm for "Jingle Bells." It has an accent called a *staccato* (marked with a dot) on the second chord of each measure.

When you play this song with Track 55, you'll use both staccato and damping. For the staccato, play a short, light chord, then quickly muffle the strings with your left hand. For the damped chord (marked with an "x"), muffle the strings *before* you strum.

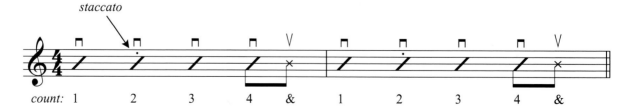

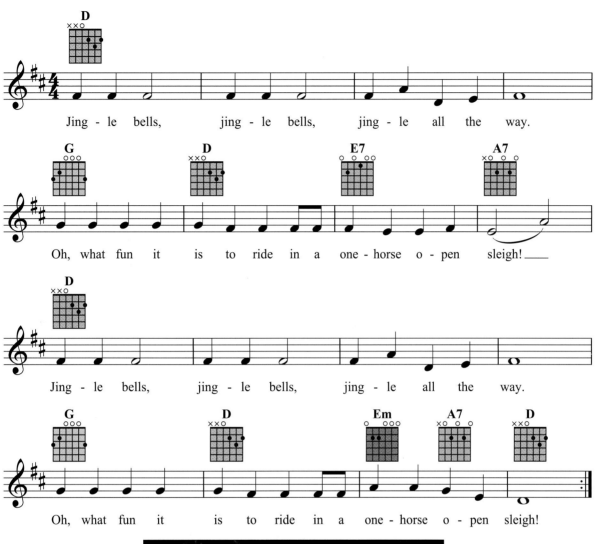

D

Jing - le bells, jing - le bells, jing - le all the way.

G **D** **E7** **A7**

Oh, what fun it is to ride in a one - horse o - pen sleigh! ____

D

Jing - le bells, jing - le bells, jing - le all the way.

G **D** **Em** **A7** **D**

Oh, what fun it is to ride in a one - horse o - pen sleigh!

Craig Nicholls of The Vines

Strum a Christmas Carol

"Silent Night" features two *suspended fourth chords.* The Dsus4 chord is just a D chord with one raised note. Moving from D to Dsus4—or from A7 to A7sus4—creates a lovely, subtle harmony.

 ## D Suspended Fourth

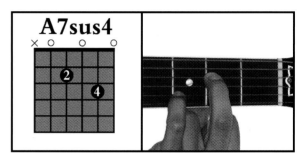

Practice moving from the D chord to Dsus4, and back again. To make this change, just add and remove your fourth finger from the first string.

 ## A7 Suspended Fourth

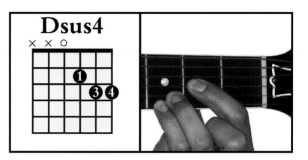

Practice moving from the A7 chord to A7sus4, and back again. To make this change, just add and remove your fourth finger from the second string.

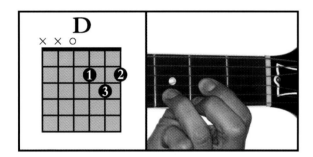

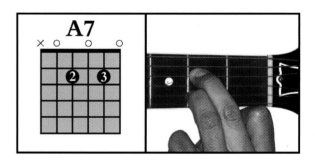

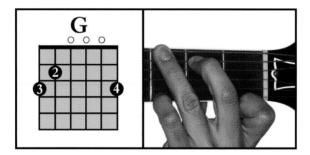

 ## Waltz Strum with Rolled Chords

Listen to this strum in Track 58, then play "Silent Night" with Track 59.

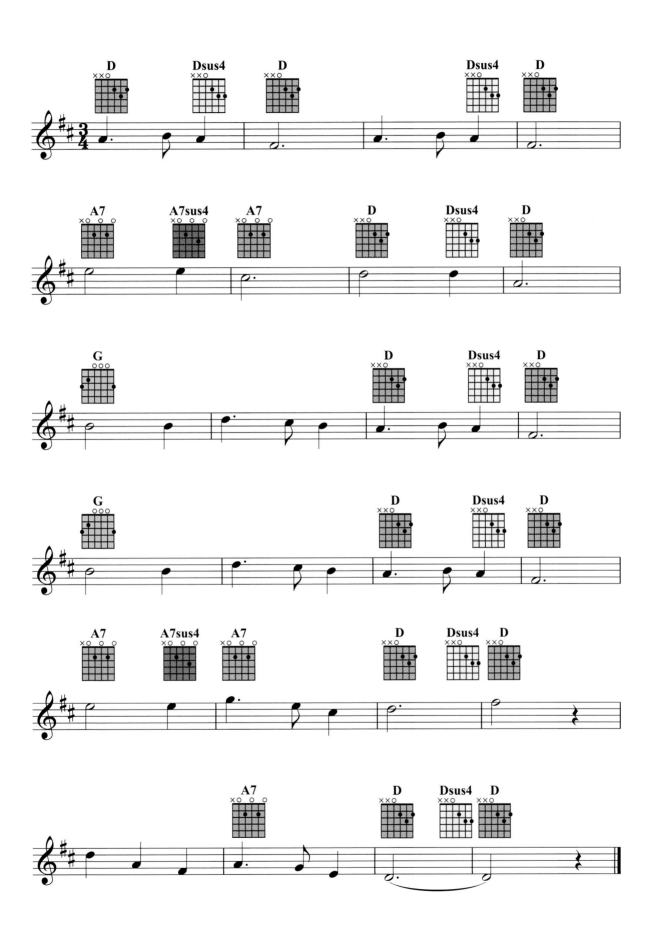

Explore a Jazz Tune

Early in her career, Ella Fitzgerald created an international sensation with her syncopated version of "A-Tisket, A-Tasket." Once you've explored the chords and strum, play this jazz standard with the CD.

 G Major Seven Chord

Strum all six strings to play this chord, but muffle Strings 1 and 5 by lightly touching them with the side of your index finger.

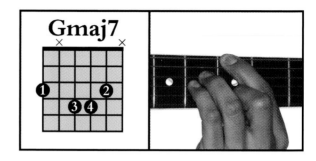

 A Minor Seven Chord

Strum the top five strings for this chord, then play this sequence: Am7-D7-Gmaj7. Note that your index finger doesn't move as you change from Am7 to D7.

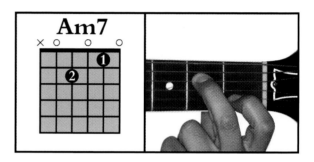

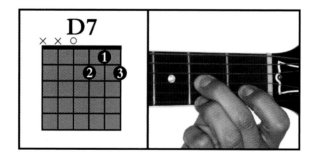

 Jazz Strum with Staccato

Listen to the guitar part on Track 62. This jazz strum features a series of staccato notes followed by a classic syncopation.

When you see the dot, remember to play a short, detached chord, then quickly muffle the strings with your left hand.

Play a Golden Oldie

"Aura Lee" enjoyed a smash revival when Elvis Presley recorded it as "Love Me Tender." Listen to the alternating bass strum, then play this great song with the CD.

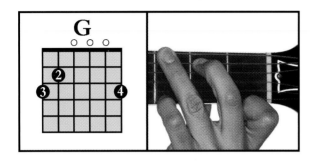

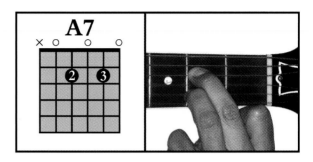

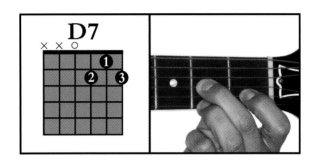

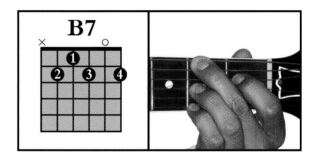

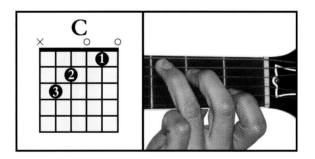

 Alternating Bass Strum

The guitar part for "Aura Lee" features two different bass notes in each bar, which adds a nice feeling of movement to the song.

As you play "Aura Lee" with Track 65, use single bass notes on the indicated strings, followed by full chords.

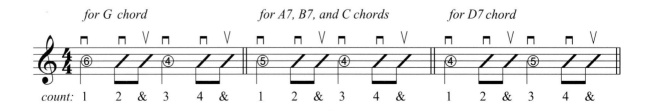

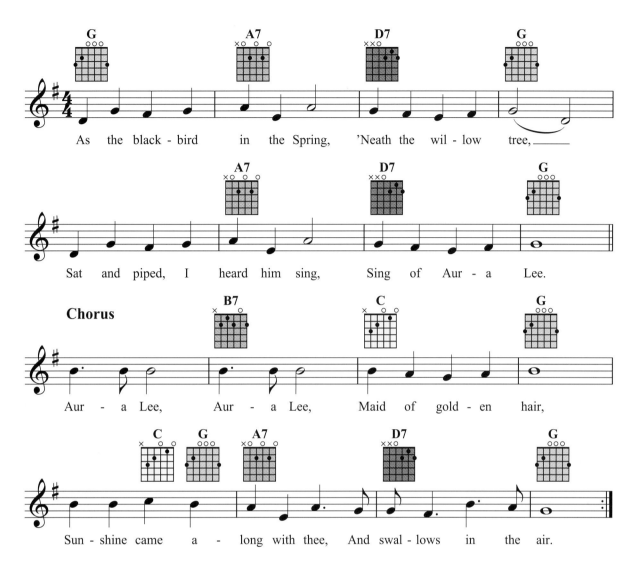

As the black-bird in the Spring, 'Neath the wil-low tree, _____

Sat and piped, I heard him sing, Sing of Aur - a Lee.

Chorus

Aur - a Lee, Aur - a Lee, Maid of gold - en hair,

Sun - shine came a - long with thee, And swal - lows in the air.

Fran Healy of Travis

Chord Dictionary

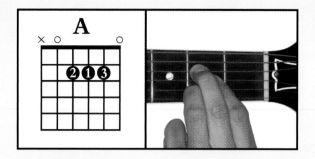

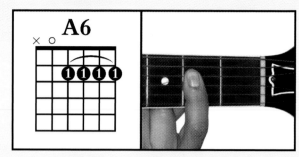

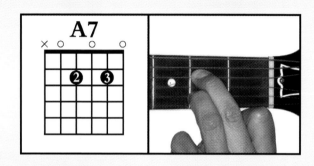

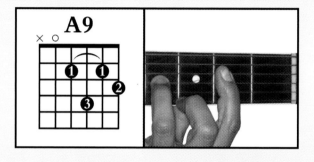

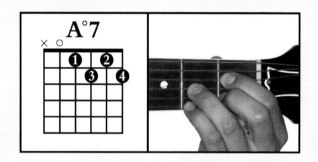

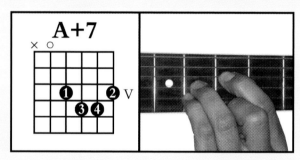

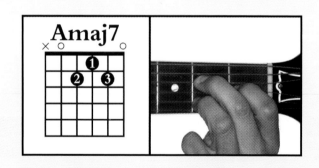

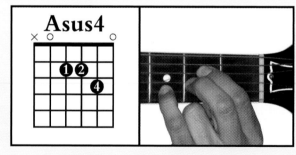

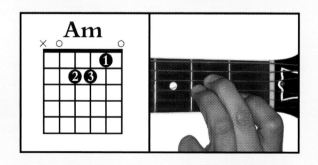

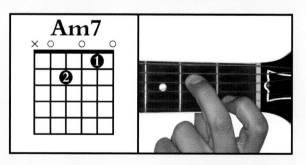

B♭
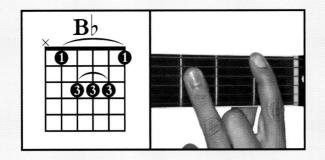

B♭6
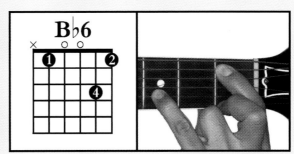

B♭7
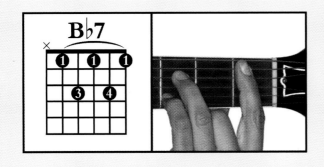

B♭9
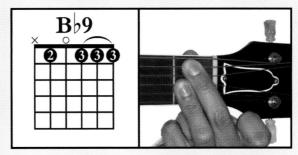

B♭°7
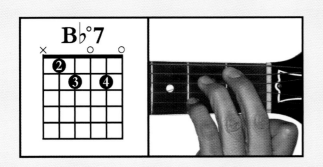

B♭+7
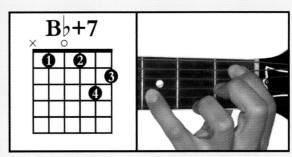

B♭maj7
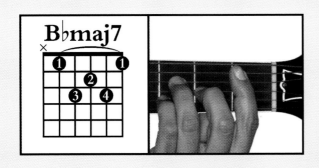

B♭sus4
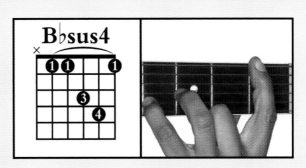

B♭m
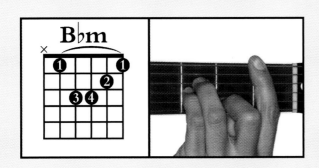

B♭m7
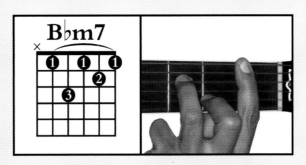

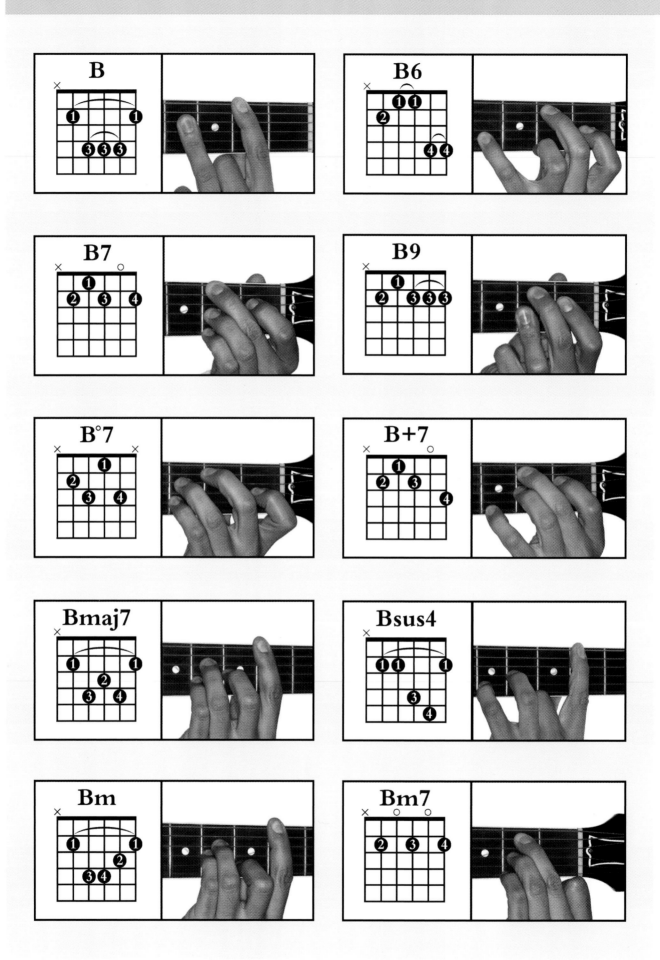

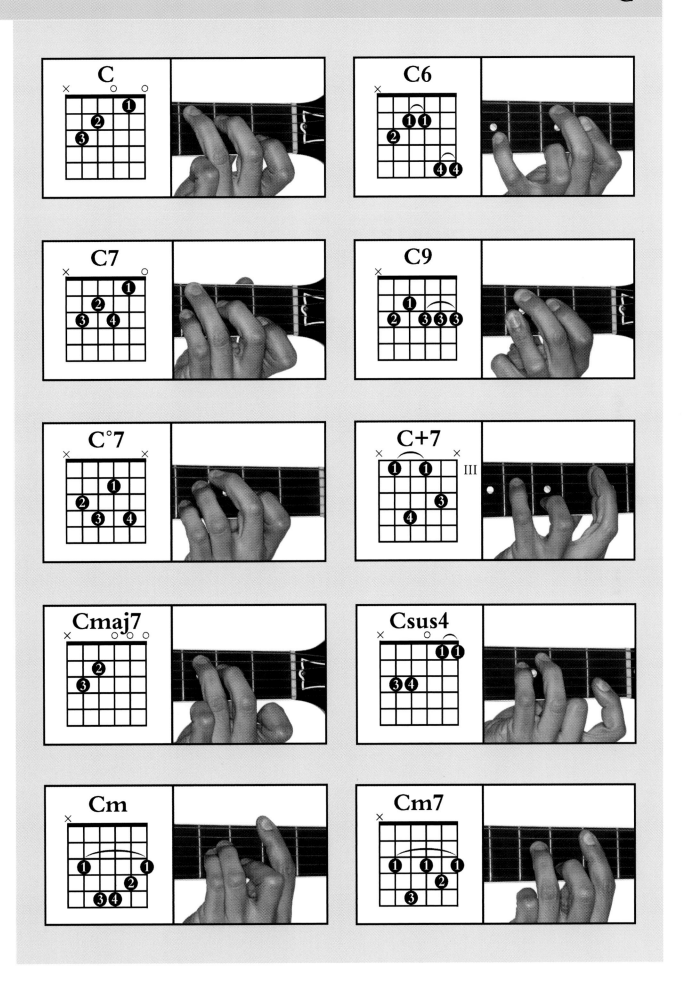

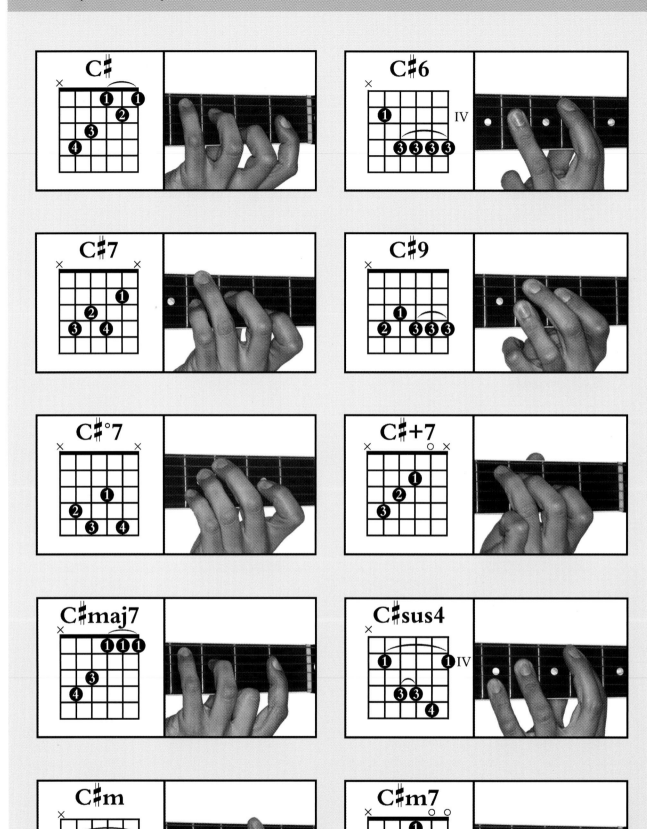

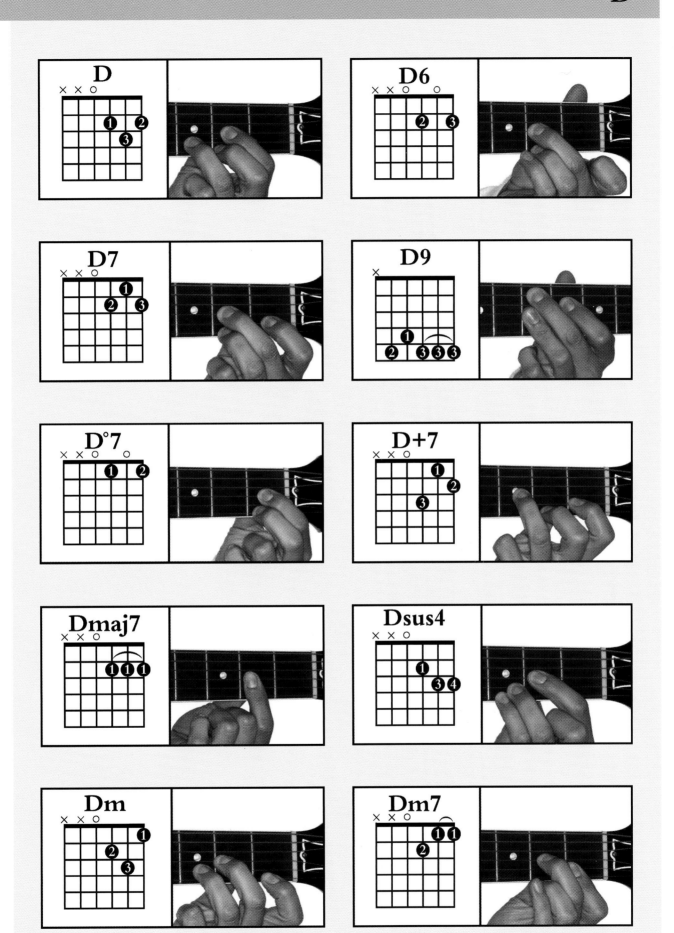

E♭ (OR D♯)

E♭
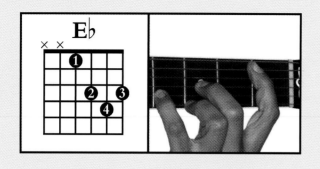

E♭6
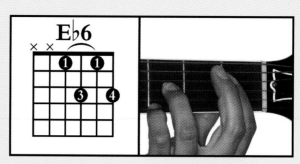

E♭7
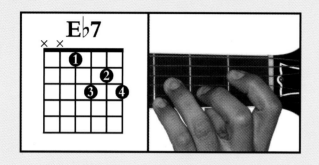

E♭9
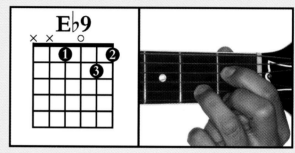

E♭°7
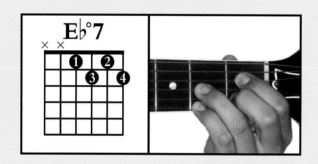

E♭+7
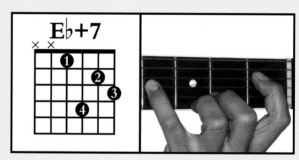

E♭maj7
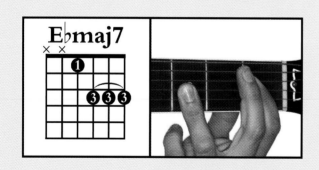

E♭sus4
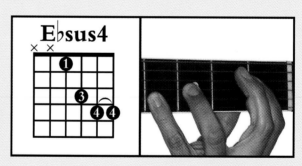

E♭m
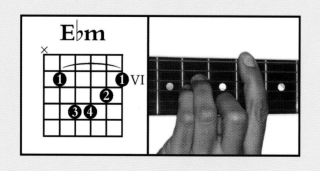

E♭m7
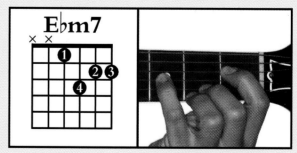

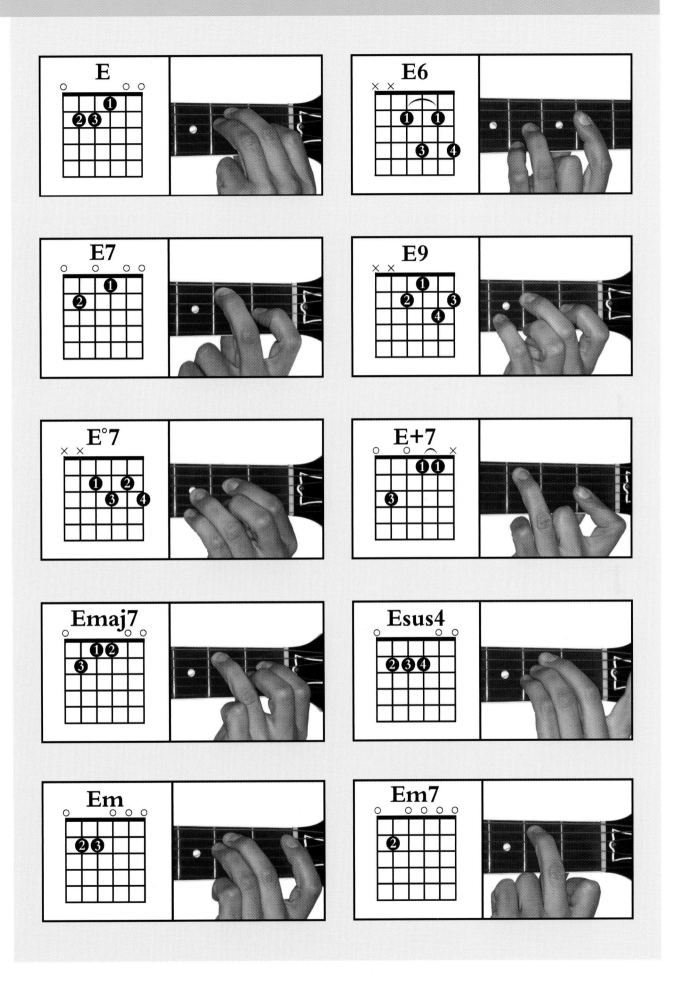

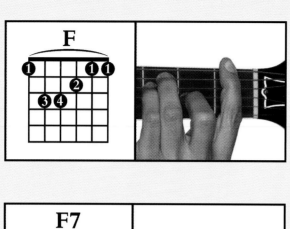

F

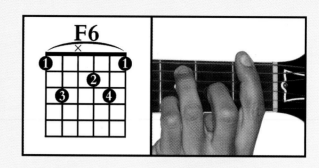

F6

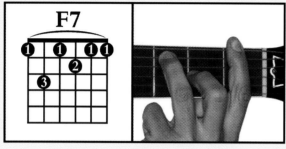

F7

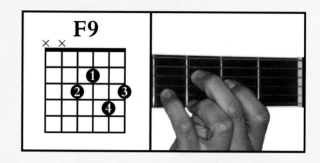

F9

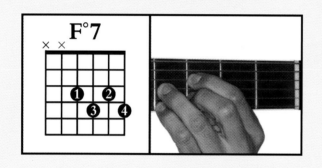

F°7

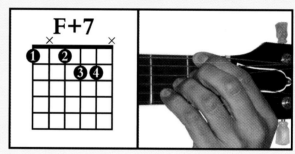

F+7

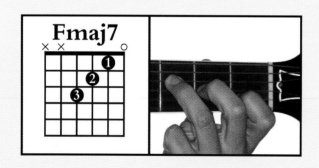

Fmaj7

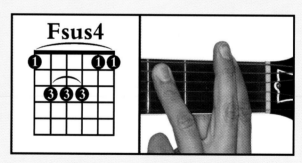

Fsus4

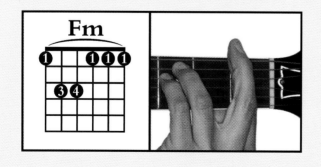

Fm

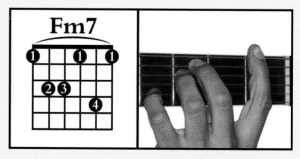

Fm7

F♯
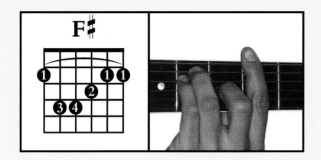

F♯6
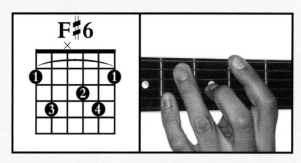

F♯7
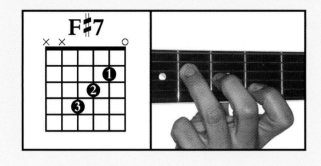

F♯9
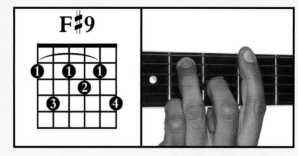

F♯°7
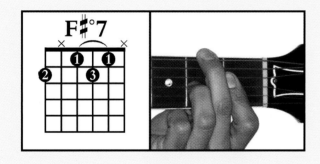

F♯+7
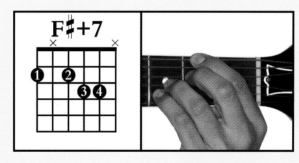

F♯maj7
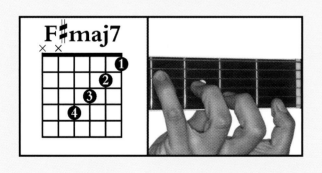

F♯sus4
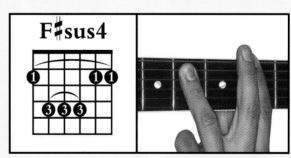

F♯m
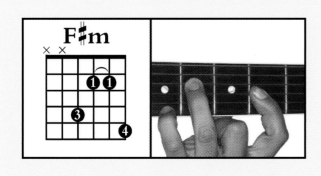

F♯m7
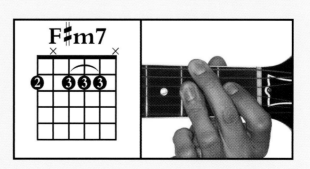

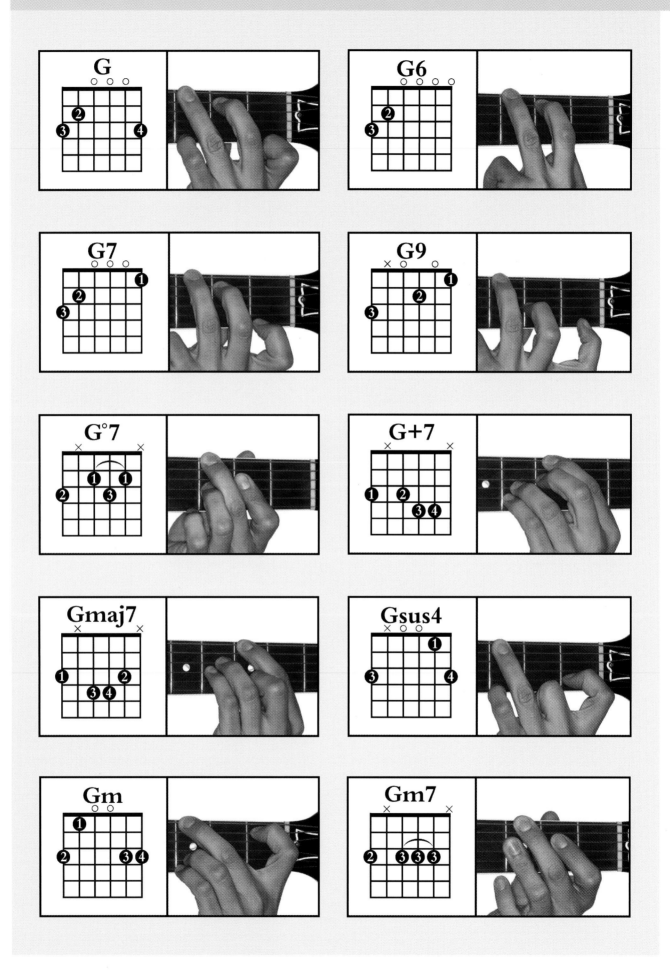

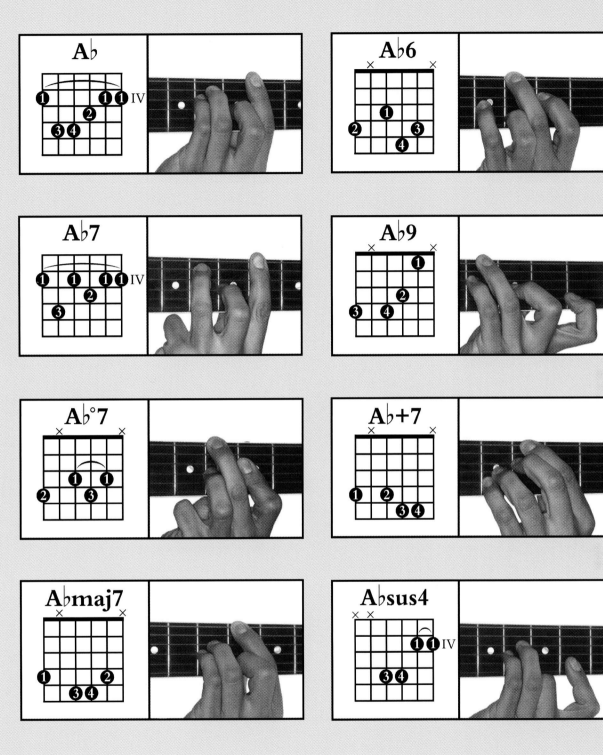

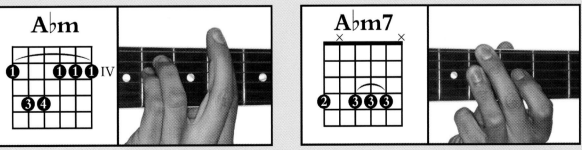

More Songs

You now have the skills to play hundreds of new songs on your own. Here's a list of classic hits you might like to add to your repertoire. Try working out the harmony to a few of these songs using the chords provided. Have fun, and keep on playing!

Achy-Breaky Heart—*Billy Ray Cyrus*
D, A7

All Right Now—*Free*
A, D, G

All Shook Up—*Elvis Presley*
A, D, E7

Born to Be Wild—*Steppenwolf*
E, G, A, D

Brown-Eyed Girl—*Van Morrison*
G, C, D7, Em

Dirty Water—*Standells*
A, D, G, C, E

Don't Worry, Be Happy—*Bobby McFerrin*
C, Dm7, F

Eleanor Rigby—*The Beatles*
Em, C

Fast Car—*Tracy Chapman*
Cmaj7, G, Em, D

Fire—*Bruce Springsteen*
G, Am, Em, C, D, A7, D7

Get It On—*T. Rex/Power Station*
A, D, C

Hero—*Enrique Iglesias*
G, Em7, C, Dsus4

Hey Joe—*Jimi Hendrix*
C, G, D, A, E7

Johnny B. Goode—*Chuck Berry*
A, D, E7

Jumping Jack Flash—*The Rolling Stones*
Verse: A, D, G
Chorus: C, G, D, A

Lady Jane—*The Rolling Stones*
D, C, G, E7, Am, D7

Lay Down Sally—*Eric Clapton*
A, D, E7

Learning to Fly—*Tom Petty*
F, C, Am, G

Losing My Religion—*R.E.M.*
F, G, Am, Em, Dm, C

Love Is All Around—*Wet Wet Wet*
G, Am, C, D

Love Me Do—*The Beatles*
A7, D7, E7

Massachusetts—*The Bee Gees*
G, Am, C, D7

Mr. Tambourine Man—*Bob Dylan*
G, A7, D

My Generation—*The Who*
A, G

Oye Como Va—*Carlos Santana*
Am7, D7

Rock and Roll—*Led Zeppelin*
A7, D7, E7

Roll Over Beethoven—*Chuck Berry*
A7, D7, E7

That'll Be the Day—*Buddy Holly/Linda Ronstadt*
C, G, D7, A7

Walk of Life—*Dire Straits*
E, A, B

When Love Comes to Town—*U2 & B.B. King*
E7, A7

Wild Thing—*The Troggs*
A, D, E, G

You Shook Me All Night Long—*AC/DC*
G, C, D

Wish You Were Here—*Pink Floyd*
Intro: Em, G, A7sus4
Verse: C, D, Am, G

Wonderful Tonight—*Eric Clapton*
G, D, C, Em